NOV -- 2011

DATE DUE JAN 0 4 2012

JUL 0 5 2012			
NOV 1 2 2013			

DEMCO 38-296

D1219185

Peabody Institute Library
Peabody, MA 01960

MATH QUEST

THE MUSEUM OF MYSTERIES

DAVID GLOVER

QEB Publishing

Illustrator: Tim Hutchinson
Editor: Lauren Taylor
Designer: Maria Bowers

Language consultants:
Penny Glover and Jenny Badee

Copyright © QEB Publishing, Inc. 2011

First published in the United States in 2011 by
QEB Publishing, Inc.
3 Wrigley, Suite A
Irvine, CA 92618

www.qed-publishing.co.uk

All rights reserved. No part of this publication may be reproduced,
stored in a retrieval system, or transmitted in any form or by any means,
electronic, mechanical, photocopying, recording, or otherwise, without the
prior permission of the publisher, nor be otherwise circulated in any form
of binding or cover other than that in which it is published and without a
similar condition being imposed on the subsequent purchaser.

ISBN 978 1 60992 086 9

Printed in China

Library of Congress Cataloging-in-Publication Data

Glover, David, 1953 Sept. 4-
 The museum of mysteries / David Glover.
   p. cm. -- (Math Quest)
 ISBN 978-1-60992-086-9 (lib. bd.)
 1. Problem solving--Juvenile literature.
 2. Museums--Juvenile literature.
 I. Title.
 QA63.G558 2012
 510.76--dc22
                        2010053360

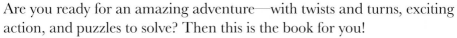
Are you ready for an amazing adventure—with twists and turns, exciting action, and puzzles to solve? Then this is the book for you!

The Museum of Mysteries is no ordinary book—you don't read the pages in order, 1, 2, 3... Instead you must jump to and fro, forwards and back, as the plot unfolds. Sometimes you may lose your way, but the story will soon guide you back to where you need to be.

The story begins on page 4. Very soon you will have problems to solve and choices to make. The choices will look something like this:

If you think the correct answer is A, go to page 10

If you think the correct answer is B, go to page 18

Your task is to solve each problem and make the right choice. So, if you think the correct answer is A, you turn to page 10 and look for the symbol. That's where you will find the next part of the story.

But what happens if you make the wrong choice? Don't worry! The text will explain where you went wrong and send you back to try again.

The problems in this quest are all about numbers. To solve them you must spot number patterns, learn about factors and prime numbers, understand place value, and recognize different properties of numbers. To help you, there is a glossary of number words at the back of the book, starting on page 44. You will find all the number ideas you need there.

As you follow the adventure, you will collect keys and other objects to put in the bag you are carrying. Make a note of the objects as you find them. You will need them all to complete the quest successfully.

So—do you think you are ready? Turn the page and let your adventure begin!

In the middle of the night you are woken up by the sound of a letter dropping through your mailbox...

> Theives are trying to steal the
> Golden Hoard at the Museum of
> Mysteries. Come quickly—there
> isn't much time!

Now you are at the Museum and are locked inside. But you're not alone—something is lurking in the shadows. You must solve the clues before the Golden Hoard, the greatest treasure of ancient times, is stolen forever! First you must collect the mystery objects, then use them to solve the final puzzle. You will need nerves of steel!

If you are ready for the challenge, go to page 17

If you are still not sure, go to page 15

 Someone has labeled the round table with numbers. But what do they mean? You search for a clue. Then you see it. It's a piece of parchment pinned to a knight's chair...

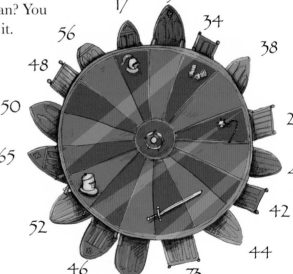

17   5
56   34
48   38
50   2
65   4
52   42
46   44
85   73

The number you need is even.
It is a multiple of five
and a factor of 100.

Look under the table,
But choose the right place,
Or you and danger will
come face to face.

If you look under number 40, go to page 30

If you look under number 50, go to page 16

4

No, this is not the largest number. You will fail to enter the burial mound with this number.

The digits in a number are highest in value on the left, and lowest on the right. Both numbers have 7 thousands and 6 hundreds. The tens are the next most valuable place. Which number has more tens?

Go to page 26

You walk up to the chest and try to lift the lid. It's locked. On the side of the chest, there is a mysterious square with numbers carved into the wood. You look closely and see that there is an inscription underneath...

Tap my lid with the magic number from my magic square.

Go to on the page with the same **number as the magic number.**

If you do not know the magic number, go to page 37

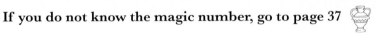

You load the arrow in the bow and point it at the dragon. But it's not scared. You shoot the arrow, but it just bounces off the dragon's body.

It was the wrong arrow! 20 is a multiple of 2 and 5, but it is not a multiple of 3. Quick—choose another arrow before it's too late!

Go to page 13

You grasp ax A. The handle starts to shake. The ax flies from your hand. Its blade just misses your head and buries itself in the wall. It's the wrong one!

The digit on the left of a number has the highest place value. The table below shows that the number 4,999 has more hundreds, tens, and ones than 5,001, but 5,001 has more thousands, so it is bigger.

Thousands	Hundreds	Tens	Ones
4	9	9	9
5	0	0	1

Go to page 32

There are 10 carved wooden boxes in Exhibit 13. They are numbered with Roman numerals, but you don't think they are in any order.

Someone has chalked some words on the table...

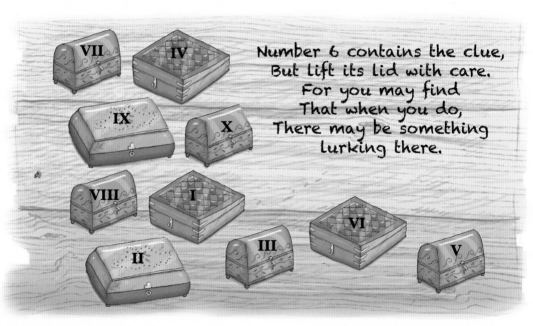

Number 6 contains the clue,
But lift its lid with care.
For you may find
That when you do,
There may be something
lurking there.

**If you lift the lid of box IV,
go to page 32**

**If you lift the lid of box VI,
go to page 34**

The passage ahead is blocked by a lifesize model of a knight with his sword raised. He looks scary—but it is only a model, isn't it?

On the wall above the knight there is a display of shields. There are more than 40 altogether. And there is something written on the first shield...

Go to page 33

In this gallery you must find Iron gloves and a disk that shines. You must seek the dragon's lair, The things you need are hidden there.

You run your finger along the number line and press the number 9. Nothing happens. You are about to turn away when you hear a loud "meow" behind you—perhaps you had better think again!

The sides of the shapes are the key. A triangle has 3 sides. A square has 4 sides, so triangle + square = 3 + 4 = 7. A hexagon has 6 sides, so square + hexagon = 4 + 6 = 10.

How many sides does a pentagon have? What is 3 + 5?

Go to page 16

You walk up to the net to take a closer look. Someone has written numbers on the wood behind. You can see them through the holes. They make a pattern, but some numbers are missing. What is special about them? And look—there's a note pinned to the net...

If the missing numbers are prime numbers, then you must search inside a Viking purse.
If the missing numbers are square numbers, then you must spy a Viking's eye

3		5	6	7	8	
13	14	15		17	18	19
23	24		26	27	28	29
33	34	35		37	38	39
43	44	45	46	47	48	
53	54	55	56	57	58	59
63		65	66	67	68	69

If you think the missing numbers are all prime numbers, go to page 38

If you think the missing numbers are all square numbers, go to page 21

You take the chainmail gloves from your bag and put them on. Now you can climb safely. You follow Pythagorpuss over the barrier and drop down on the other side.

Go to page 38

That's correct! There are 242 beads in the necklace. The clue told you to add the digits together. $2 + 4 + 2 = 8$. That's where you go, Exhibit 8, "Swords."

There are three swords in a dusty cabinet. The dates when the swords were made are printed on display cards. Someone has written a message in the dust.

> Take the oldest sword with you,
> It will show you what to do.

If you choose sword A, go to page 23

If you choose sword B, go to page 13

If you choose sword C, go to page 23

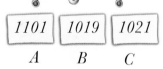

| 1101 | 1019 | 1021 |
| A | B | C |

You have chosen the correct mosaic! As you step on the mosaic you hear ancient machinery rumble and groan. The mosaic starts to rise. You are carried up until your eyes are level with a stone plaque high on the wall.

Go to page 31

You see a message carved on the horn...

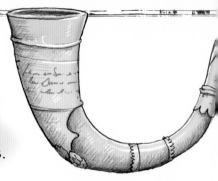

Blow me carefully for a sign,
Blow me exactly three squared times.

**If you blow the horn 6 times,
go to page 42**

**If you blow the horn 9 times,
go to page 12**

The galleries are dark and eerie. A red light flashing inside a display case attracts your attention. You see two vases inside the case. They are numbered 24 and 25, and someone has taped a card to the display...

*Choose a vase if you dare,
Five times five holds the clue.
But be sure you choose with care,
If you're wrong, it's the end for you!*

If you choose vase 24, go to page 26

If you choose vase 25, go to page 27

You've chosen the wrong shield! The Viking warrior comes to life. He swings his ax toward you. But you use the shield to block the blow. The warrior crumbles into dust on the ground.

The digit after the decimal point is "tenths."
The decimal 0.6 means six tenths or $\frac{6}{10}$.
Which shield has ten parts, six of which are red?

Go to page 30

You search around for a wooden stool. It's next to the tiller at the stern! That's where the Viking chieftain sat as he sailed with his crew.

    You feel underneath the stool. There's something fixed with a nail. It's the golden pendant the chieftain wore for luck—his precious amulet!
You made the right choice!

Go to page 39

At the end of the passageway there are two doors in the wall. It looks like there are signs pinned to them. The next instruction on the scroll says to "look for the truth." You step closer and read the notices pinned to the doors...

A

When you divide an even number by two, the answer is always an odd number.

B

When you double an odd number, the answer is always an even number.

If you think the sign on door A is true, go to page 27

If you think the sign on door B is true, go to page 22

You blew the correct number! You see a flicker of light from an oil lamp right at the front of the boat, where a carving of a wolf's head stands. You climb forward to get a closer look.

Go to page 39

It's the right shield! Underneath there is a folded piece of paper. It's a map of the gallery.

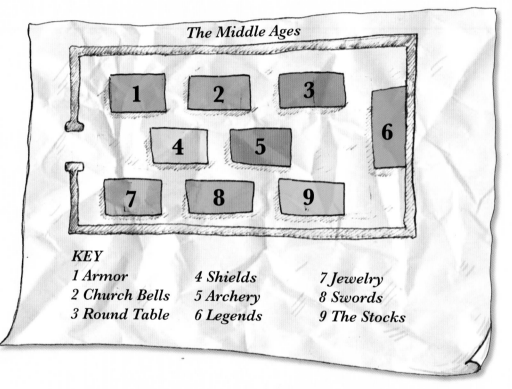

The Middle Ages

1   2   3   6

4   5

7   8   9

KEY
1 Armor
2 Church Bells
3 Round Table

4 Shields
5 Archery
6 Legends

7 Jewelry
8 Swords
9 The Stocks

But where is the dragon's lair? It isn't shown in the key. You turn the map over. There is another clue on the back.

To find the next place in your quest, visit the highest prime number in the list.

If you think you should visit Exhibit 7, go to page 23

If you think you should visit Exhibit 9, go to page 41

As you reach for the sword it jumps into your hand! It's the right one! In the cabinet, you now notice a silk scarf folded where the sword stood. Stitched into the cloth you find a message...

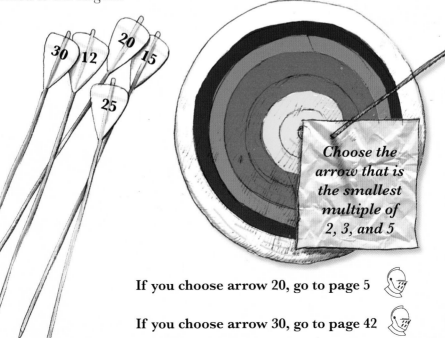

To draw the dragon from his lair,
Ring the bell that is not square,
Then place the arrow in a bow,
And he will take you
down below.

So you must ring a bell. With the sword in your hand, you head for Exhibit 2, "Church Bells."

Go to page 17

There is a bow and a display of arrows at the exhibit. Each arrow is numbered. But which should you use? Then you see an instruction pinned to the target...

Choose the arrow that is the smallest multiple of 2, 3, and 5

If you choose arrow 20, go to page 5

If you choose arrow 30, go to page 42

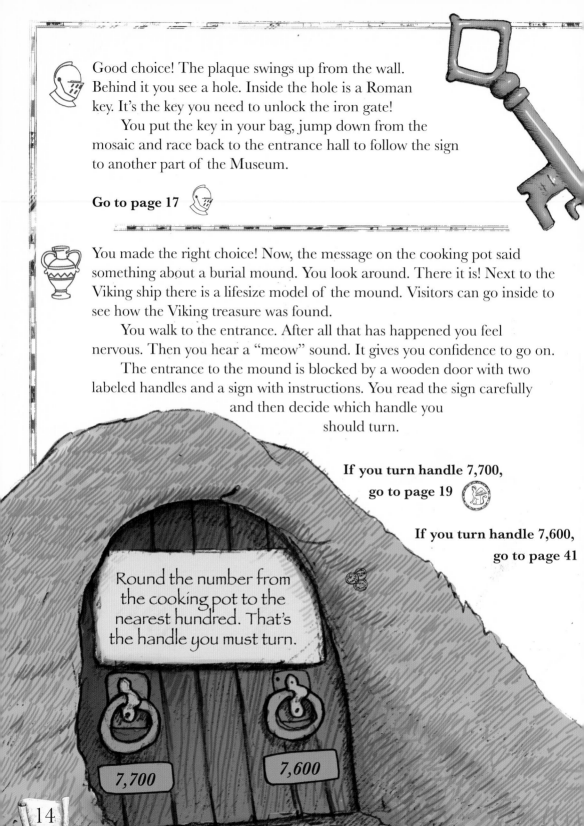

Good choice! The plaque swings up from the wall. Behind it you see a hole. Inside the hole is a Roman key. It's the key you need to unlock the iron gate!

You put the key in your bag, jump down from the mosaic and race back to the entrance hall to follow the sign to another part of the Museum.

Go to page 17

You made the right choice! Now, the message on the cooking pot said something about a burial mound. You look around. There it is! Next to the Viking ship there is a lifesize model of the mound. Visitors can go inside to see how the Viking treasure was found.

You walk to the entrance. After all that has happened you feel nervous. Then you hear a "meow" sound. It gives you confidence to go on.

The entrance to the mound is blocked by a wooden door with two labeled handles and a sign with instructions. You read the sign carefully and then decide which handle you should turn.

If you turn handle 7,700, go to page 19

If you turn handle 7,600, go to page 41

Round the number from the cooking pot to the nearest hundred. That's the handle you must turn.

7,700

7,600

14

Don't be afraid. It's a challenging adventure, but help is nearby. When you get stuck, a mysterious friend will guide you. Just follow the instructions one at a time, and see how far you get.

Now, get on your way to the entrance hall. Good luck.

Go to page 17

You're right! The numbers in each row, column, and diagonal of a magic square always add up to the same magic number. The magic number for this square is 15.

RED—SOUND ALARM
BLUE—CLOSE SHUTTERS
BLACK—TURN OFF POWER

You tap 15 times on the lid and it opens. Inside there is a small clay tablet covered with strange writing. You don't know what it means, but you think it might be important. You put the tablet in your bag. And wait—there's something written on the bottom of the chest!

> *Now retrace your steps if you can,*
> *Back to where you began.*
> *But look for patterns you can see,*
> *You still haven't found*
> *The Roman key.*

Go to page 22

Oh no! You've chosen the wrong pattern. There are 16 squares altogether and 7 are white. That's less than half.

The mosaic crumbles beneath your feet. You start to fall into a bottomless pit. At the last moment, you grab the bottom of a nearby curtain. Slowly you haul yourself out of the hole. The pieces of the mosaic move back into place.

Go to page 35

Exhibit 20 is a display about Greek mathematics. Different shapes, words, and a row of numbers are carved in a stone tablet. There is a display card below it—it looks like a puzzle.

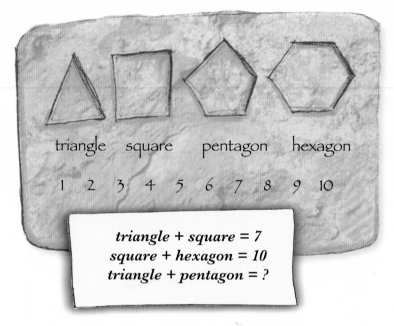

triangle   square   pentagon   hexagon

1 2 3 4 5 6 7 8 9 10

triangle + square = 7
square + hexagon = 10
triangle + pentagon = ?

You decide you must work out the missing number.

If you think the number is 8, go to page 36

If you think the number is 9, go to page 8

You crawl under the table. A pair of chainmail gloves lies on the floor. Iron gloves! You've chosen the correct number!

You put the gloves in your bag. Then you see a fierce hunting dog with its back to you on the other side of the table. You jump back quickly before it spots you.

Now you have the things you need. You race to the entrance hall as fast as you can to follow the directions to another part of the Museum.

Go to page 17

There is a row of ancient bells at the exhibit. But which one should you ring? None of the bells are square—they are bell-shaped. Then you see the numbers engraved on the bells. The clue meant to ring a bell that isn't a square number! Which bell isn't a square number?

If you ring bell 32, go to page 36

If you ring bell 36, go to page 33

You are standing in the main entrance hall. Four corridors lead in different directions. You must choose which one to take. But look! There are muddy footprints leading down the corridor to the Golden Hoard. You see the beam from a flashlight. That's where the thieves have gone! Which part of the Museum should you visit?

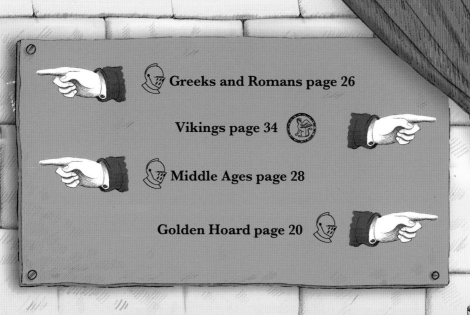

Greeks and Romans page 26

Vikings page 34

Middle Ages page 28

Golden Hoard page 20

You take the amulet from your bag. On the back there is an inscription.

You enter the digits 879, and the door opens.

Go to page 43

Found in East Anglia. Date around 879 A.D.

You climb aboard the ship. There is a torn slip of paper pinned to one of the ropes. It's the next instruction!

> **Use the ax to cut a rope.**
> **The number of the rope to pick**
> **is a multiple of 1, 2, 3, 4, and 6.**

There are 20 ropes altogether. But which is the right one?

If you cut rope 12, go to page 31

If you cut rope 18, go to page 41

You are correct! You tap 10 times.

   The wolf's eyes glow bright red. They shine like two laser beams onto an object in the distance. It's a huge iron cooking pot like a witch's cauldron. You climb down from the boat and walk up to the pot.

Go to page 26

Ahead the corridor is blocked by a pile of spiked balls. The burglars must have have piled them there so they couldn't be followed. There's no way through!

   But look—Pythagorpuss sees a way! He leaps to the top where there is a gap. But you can't follow. The spikes are too sharp. They will cut your hands. Then you see a message chalked on the ground…

> Chainmail gloves
> will get you up,
> Then you can climb
> and not be cut.

   Knights wore chainmail in the Middle Ages!

If you have the chainmail gloves, go to page 9

If you do not have the gloves, you need to visit the Middle Ages exhibition. Go to page 17

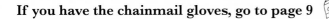

You've chosen the right number. 7,651 is closer to 7,700 than to 7,600 (the "tens" digit is 5 or more) so you round up the hundreds digit.

   The door swings open. You step bravely forward.

Go to page 30

You follow the footprints along the corridor. You come to a locked iron gate and can't go any farther.

But look—there's a brass plate on the gate that has an inscription…

To unlock this gate you need a Roman key.

If you have the key, go to page 27

If you do not have the key, you need to visit the Greeks and Romans section of the Musuem. Go to page 17

Should you climb down the stairs? Not sure what to do, you read the next instruction on the scroll…

*Climb down,
But climb with care.
The thieves have
Set traps for you.
But which stairs are
safe—and where?
Count in threes
Is what you do.*

You work out that you must only step on the stairs in the sequence 3, 6, 9… But will you step on stair number 16?

If you are going to step on stair 16, go to page 32

If you are not going to step on stair 16, go to page 28

Yes—the numbers are all square numbers!

A Viking's eye—where could that be? Then you see it. There's a giant eye shape painted on the ship's sail. You climb back onboard to take a closer look.

Go to page 36

The dragon curls up in a corner and watches suspiciously as you explore.

At the back of the cave you find a trapdoor. "Look beneath the dragon's lair…"—this must be it!

There is an iron handle on the trapdoor, but it will not budge. Then you see another clue carved into the wood...

I am 56.
Find half of me.
Find half of me again.
And once more.
What do you find?
Turn my handle that
number of times.

If you turn the handle 6 times, go to page 40

If you turn the handle 7 times, go to page 40

You open the door and step into a small room. There is a large wooden chest in the corner.

　　The notice was true. The doubles of odd numbers are all even numbers.

Number	1	3	5	7	9	11
Double	2	6	10	14	18	22

Go to page 5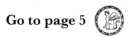

You turn and retrace your steps. Through the door, along the passage, up the steps (three at a time) and back into the Greek and Roman galleries.

　　But what was that about patterns? As you head back toward the main entrance hall you see a sign, pointing in the direction of the Mosaic Exhibition. Mosaics—they are patterns! You turn in the direction of the sign. There's that purring sound again … what could it be?

Go to page 35

Nothing happens. You pushed the wrong number! The diagram below shows where 100 is on the line. The number 99 is only 1 less than 100. It is just less than halfway between 0 and 200. The machinery reverses. The mosaic starts to drop.

　　Quick, try again before it's too late!

Go to page 31

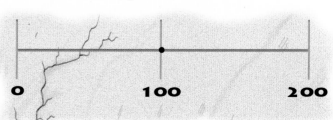

You follow the map to Exhibit 7. You were correct, 7 is the highest prime number between 1 and 9.

The cabinet at Exhibit 7 contains a beautiful beaded necklace. Something is written on the glass...

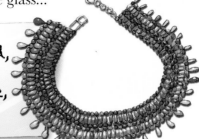

To find a number you will need,
You must count every bead.
Then add the digits one by one,
That's the place you must run.

But there are hundreds of beads in the necklace! You do not have time to count them all—the thieves must be getting close to the hoard! But then you spot a printed card...

Necklace made with 10 blue beads for each red bead.
Number of red beads = 22

Now you can work out the number!

If you think the number of beads is 222, go to page 37

If you think the number is 242, go to page 9

As you reach for the sword a loud "meow" makes you jump back. The sword topples. Its point sticks in the floor, just where you had been standing. It was the wrong sword!
The oldest sword will have the smallest number for its date.

Go to page 9

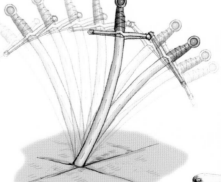

The police storm in and arrest the thieves. The Golden Hoard is safe! The chief of police pats you on the back and smiles. "Congratulations," he says. "You're a hero!"

Maybe he's right, but suddenly you feel very sleepy. It has been a tiring adventure! You can't wait to collapse into a chair with Pythagorpuss on your lap.

THE END

You follow the sign to the Greek and Roman galleries. You pause for a moment. Are those soft footsteps following you? For some reason you don't feel afraid.

Go to page 10

There is an inscription around the top of the pot...

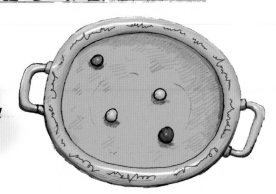

Thousands, hundreds, tens, and ones. Find the biggest number to open the burial mound.

Look—there's something inside the pot. You reach inside and pull out four beads. Each bead has a digit scratched on it.

You think that the beads are the thousands, hundreds, tens, and ones the inscription refers to. But which is which? You need the biggest number, so you arrange the beads to make the largest number possible.

If you think that the biggest number is 7,615, go to page 5

If you think that the biggest number is 7,651, go to page 14

You put your hand in the vase. Something hairy crawls over your fingers! You snatch your hand away. A giant tarantula climbs out of the vase. You were lucky it didn't bite you!

You chose the wrong vase: "five times five" is 25, not 24.

Go to page 10

You put your hand in the vase and feel around. It's the right vase!
You find six clay disks and a slip of paper with some instructions...

Put the disks in order, smallest first.
Where should the blank disc go?
Find the exhibit with the missing number.

Go to page 42

You open the door and step into a small room. But something is wrong! You cannot breathe! You just manage to return through the door before you pass out.

The notice on the door was false. For example, half of 4 is 2, which is an even number.

Go to page 11

You take the Roman key from your bag. It turns in the lock. The gate is stiff, and creaks loudly as you open it, but you are through.

Someone follows you through the gate. You look down at your feet. It's Pythagorpuss, the Museum cat! He has been helping you all along! Now you can face the challenges together.

Go to page 19

You descend safely to the bottom of the stairs, three steps at a time. As you climb down you see the tripwire the thieves have set on step 16.

At the bottom of the stairs you find a passageway lit by flickering flames.

Go to page 11

You are right. The rule for the number sequence on the disks is "add 4." The sequence is 1, 5, 9, 13, 17, 21.

You walk around the gallery looking for Exhibit 13. But you can't find it. Then, in the darkest corner of the room, you see two bright eyes shining. Somehow the eyes seem friendly, so you walk toward them. There it is—Exhibit 13!

Go to page 6

You follow the sign to the exhibits of the Middle Ages. You see suits of armor lining the walls and shields with coats of arms on display. At any moment you expect a king and his courtiers to walk in a procession along the corridor.

Wait a moment— what's that? Are those eyes shining out at you from the darkness?

Go to page 7

You hold the clay tablet up to the mirror. Its message becomes clear...

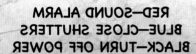

RED—SOUND ALARM
BLUE—CLOSE SHUTTERS
BLACK—TURN OFF POWER

Now you know the sequence! You press the blue button. The shutters come down and the thieves are trapped. You press the black button. The sound of drilling stops—the Hoard is safe! Finally you press the red button. The alarm goes off. The police are on their way!

Go to page 24

You look around for a splendid bed. It's not on the ship, but then you see it next to the skeleton. It was buried with the chieftain.

You jump from the ship and rush to the bed. There is nothing on top, so you crawl underneath. But something is wrong! Vines carved in the bed's legs start to come to life, writhing and wrapping themselves around your wrists and ankles. You tear yourself free and escape just in time.

You were wrong about the colors. The eye is 25 % green and 40 % red, that's 65 % for those colours. The rest of the eye is blue. 100 % − 65 % = 35 %, so the eye is more red (40 %) than blue (35 %).

Go to page 36

Inside the mound the displays are brightly lit. Dummies dressed as Vikings stand around the body of the Viking chief. A voice from a loudspeaker tells the story of the burial. Wait a minute, what is the voice saying now? It seems to be talking to you!

"Look beneath a Viking shield,
find the shield that's 0.6 red.
Six tenths in other words."

You look at the shields the Vikings carry. They are all painted red and blue. Which one should you choose?

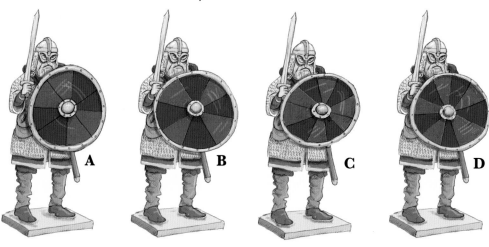

If you choose shield B, go to page 10

If you choose shield C, go to page 33

You duck under the table and come face to face with a fierce hunting dog. He's going to attack! Then a dark shape runs under the table and distracts him. You make a quick exit!

You chose the wrong number and nearly paid the price! The number 40 is even and a multiple of 5, but it is not a factor of 100.

Go to page 4

You see Exhibit 14 immediately. It's a huge stone column from a temple. As you walk toward it, it starts to topple! Watch out! A ball of fur leaps at your chest and knocks you sideways. The column crashes to the ground—just where you had been standing. Who or what pushed you out of the way?

You chose the wrong number. The rule for the number sequence on the discs is "add 4." The sequence is 1, 5, 9, 13, 17, 21.

Go to page 42

You read the inscription on the plaque...

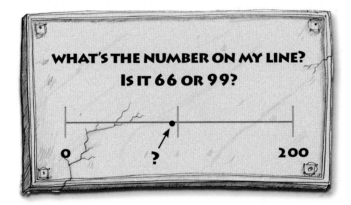

WHAT'S THE NUMBER ON MY LINE?
IS IT 66 OR 99?

0   ?   200

If you press 66,
go to page 22

If you press 99,
go to page 14

It's the right rope! Rope 12 goes to the top of the ship's mast. It is holding something up there. You cut the rope and, as if by magic, all the ropes fall away and a strange object slides down the mast. It's a huge horn. The Vikings blew the horn to warn of their approach.

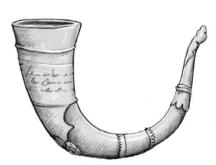

Go to page 10

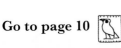

You've chosen the wrong box! As you lift the lid you hear a loud buzzing sound. An enormous wasp zooms out, heading straight for your neck. It's going to sting you!

You duck into the shadows under the table. Confused, the wasp flies away toward a moonlit window.

These are the Roman numerals for the numbers 1 to 10. The numeral for 6 is VI not IV.

1	2	3	4	5	6	7	8	9	10
I	II	III	IV	V	VI	VII	VIII	IX	X

Go to page 6

You look around at the axes on display. They are labeled with their weights in grams.

Ax A
four thousand, nine hundred, and ninety

Ax B
five thousand and one

If you think axe A is heavier, go to page 6

If you think axe B is heavier, go to page 38

If you step on number 16 you will fall into the burglars' trap!

You must count in threes to find which steps are safe: 3, 6, 9, 12, 15, 18, 21... Step 16 is not in the list.

Go to page 20

You strike the bell with the sword. It does not ring —it is cracked! Out from the crack slides a brightly colored snake. It's going to bite your foot! Then, like a flash, something shadowy pounces on the snake's tail. The snake slithers back inside the bell. You chose the wrong bell! $6 \times 6 = 36$. 36 is a square number.

Go to page 17

It's the right shield! You lift it down from the dummy and turn it over. Underneath it is a piece torn from an ancient map. You don't know if you will need it, but you put it in your bag.

There's also a message on the back of the shield...

 You are winning this dangerous game. Now head back from whence you came. But look for numbers in a net, You have to find the amulet!

Go to page 39

Iron gloves and a shiny disk? Where could they be? You glance at the second shield and see another message. It's an instruction...

If you lift shield 29, go to page 37

If you lift shield 28, go to page 12

Lift the shield halfway between 25 and 31. But beware if you are wrong, you will need some armor on!

You've chosen the correct box! Inside is an ancient scroll. It's tied with a strip of leather. You untie the knot and the scroll unrolls. It seems to be a list of numbers and instructions. You keep the scroll with you— you're bound to need the instructions soon.

The first line is just a single number. You guess that you must find Exhibit 20 next.

You set off cautiously in that direction. Wait a minute—is that purring you can hear? Feeling encouraged, you move more quickly.

Go to page 16

You walk along the corridor toward the Vikings' gallery. Someone has left a dish of milk near a pillar. You hear a purring sound and glimpse the tip of a tail.

Ahead you see a Viking ship. It is surrounded by displays of swords, axes, horned helmets, and jewelry, dug up from a burial mound. A trail of milky paw prints leads you to a glass box. Inside the box there is a human skeleton. It is the Viking chief. A card on the display gives a chilling message...

> The amulet you must seek,
> Was hidden beneath this Viking's seat,
> But be careful in your quest,
> The Viking curse won't let you rest!
> The chieftain's ax is what you need,
> The heaviest of all will succeed.

A cold wind whistles through the galleries and ruffles the ship's sails…

Go to page 32

You take the three items from your bag and lay them on the desk. You have a golden mirror, a clay tablet covered with mystery writing, and a scrap torn from a map.

Wait a minute—a map gives you directions! You look more closely at the tiny letters on the scrap. You can only just make out what they say...

The mystery writing will be clear, When you see it in the mirror.

Now you understand! The writing on the tablet must be mirror writing—it's back to front!

Go to page 29

There are two mosaics on the floor ahead. They are different patterns, but what are you supposed to do? You look at the next instruction on the scroll...

Step on the pattern that's half white. But beware, if you are wrong, you're in for a fright!

A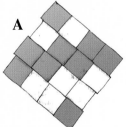

B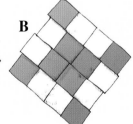

If you step on mosaic A, go to page 15

If you step on mosaic B, go to page 9

Yes! This is correct. Now that you know the number, you are prepared for the next challenge. Remember, the number is 7,651. You might want to write it down.

Go to page 14

You run your finger along the number line and press the number 8. The stone tablet begins to shake. You stand back. It falls to the floor with a crash and reveals the entrance to a secret passageway. Narrow stairs descend into a lamplit passage.

The shapes' sides were the key:
A triangle has 3 sides.
A square has 4 sides.
So triangle + square = 3 + 4 = 7.

You were correct to work out the answer as 8. A pentagon has 5 sides, so triangle + pentagon = 3 + 5 = 8.

Go to page 20

You strike the bell with the sword. It rings loudly. It's the right bell—32 is not a square number.

A huge head emerges slowly from the cave mouth at the Exhibit of Legends. The dragon is looking right at you! Now you need a bow and arrow. You race to Exhibit 5, "Archery."

Go to page 13

Tiny writing at the center of the eye reveals the next clue...

If you are looking for a stool, go to page 11

If you are looking for a bed, go to page 29

I'm 25 % green and 40 % red,
The rest of me is blue.
If you think I'm more red than blue,
Find a simple wooden stool.
If I'm more blue than red,
Lie in a chieftain's splendid bed.

You've chosen the wrong shield! The knight in armor walks toward you swinging his sword. But then a ball of fur dashes between his legs. He trips and crashes to the floor.

You should have chosen the 28th shield. This diagram shows that 28 is halfway between 25 and 31.

25   26   27   28   29   30   31

Go to page 33

The numbers in each row of a magic square always add up to the same "magic number." The numbers in the columns and diagonals add up to the magic number, too. Check for yourself.

$$\begin{array}{|c|c|c|} \hline 2 & 7 & 6 \\ \hline 9 & 5 & 1 \\ \hline 4 & 3 & 8 \\ \hline \end{array}$$

$2 + 7 + 6 = 15$

$9 + 5 + 1 = 15$

$4 + 3 + 8 = 15$

Go to page 5

You think there are 222 beads in the necklace. The clue told you to add the digits together. $2 + 2 + 2 = 6$. You think you must go to Exhibit 6, "Legends."

The exhibit looks like the mouth of a cave. You feel afraid. You can smell sulfur fumes. Huge yellow eyes are watching you from the darkness! Suddenly a tongue of flame explodes toward you—it's a dragon! You run for cover. You have found the dragon's lair, but you can't get close.

Your answer to the last clue was wrong! There are 22 red beads, so there are 220 blue beads. How many beads are there in all?

Go to page 23

You look around for a Viking purse. You see it in a cabinet next to the skeleton. It's a leather bag tied at the neck.

    You take down the purse but something feels wrong. Is something moving inside? Carefully you untie the neck, but before you can put your hand inside, something crawls out. It's a scorpion! You throw the bag and the scorpion as far away as you can.

    You were wrong. The missing numbers are 4, 9, 16, 25, 36, 49, 64.
They are all square numbers.

Go to page 8

You can hear the sound of drilling ahead. The thieves have raised the steel safety shutters from the exhibition doors. Now they are breaking into the safe that holds the treasure at night. Why hasn't the alarm gone off?

    Pythagorpuss knows what to do. He runs to a door marked "Museum Office." But there is a combination lock on the door. You cannot get in! Then you see a yellow sticky note next to the keypad...

The combination has been set,
To the date of the Viking amulet.

If you have the amulet, go to page 18

If you do not have the amulet, you need to visit the Vikings section. Go to page 17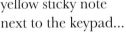

It's the right ax! On the ax head you see an instruction...

Take me aboard
the Viking ship

Go to page 18

Now that you have the amulet, you can continue your adventure to another part of the Museum. You race back to the entrance hall to follow the sign, but someone else is with you!

Go to page 17

The flickering light shines on a small card inside the wolf's mouth. It's another instruction!

> Count the wolf's teeth one by one,
> Tap the number when you're done.
> If you're right he'll lead you on,
> If you're wrong, he'll see you gone.
>
> The number of the wolf's teeth
> is a factor of 20.

If the wolf could have 10 teeth, go to page 19

If the wolf could have 12 teeth, go to page 43

You retrace your steps to the door of the burial mound. Watching for Vikings, you step back into the gallery and head for the door. But what was that about a net? Then you see it. There is a fishing net hanging over the side of the ship.

Go to page 8

You turn the handle 7 times and pull. It's the right number! The trapdoor swings open.

Inside there is a round mirror with a gold frame—a disk that shines! It's fit for a princess. You put the mirror in your bag.

Pinned to the underside of the trapdoor you find a page from an ancient book...

> *Now that you've found*
> *the disk that shines,*
> *Do not waste your precious time.*
> *The gloves you need can be found,*
> *Where the Knights all sit around.*

Where do the Knights sit around? A round table, of course! You dash from the dragon's lair to the Round Table Exhibit.

Go to page 4

You turn the handle 6 times, but the trapdoor is still locked shut!

Half of 56 is 28. Half of 28 is 14. What is half of 14?

Quickly, try again before the dragon gets restless!

Go to page 21

You cut rope 18, but it's the wrong one! The sail falls on top of you. Ropes wrap around your arms and legs. You are trapped!

Then you feel something pulling at the ropes with sharp teeth and claws—suddenly you are free again!

Twelve is a multiple of 1, 2, 3, 4, and 6. Eighteen is a multiple of 1, 2, 3, and 6, but not of 4. All the multiples of 4 are given by the 4 times table: 4, 8, 12, 16, 20, and so on. Eighteen is not in this sequence.

Go to page 18

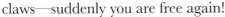

The handle will not turn. You've chosen the wrong number!

From behind the door you hear the sound of a Viking horn and running feet. Quickly you duck behind the cooking pot. The door bursts open and a fierce Viking ghost rushes out, waving his sword. He charges across the room and disappears into the Viking ship. The door slams behind him.

To round 7,651 to the nearest hundred, look at the "tens" digit. Is it 5 or more? If it is, then round up the hundreds digit.

Go to page 14

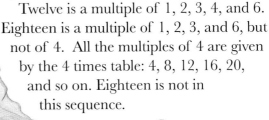

You follow the map to Exhibit 9, "The Stocks." You can't see a clue so you examine the stocks carefully. As you lean over, the stocks snap shut, trapping your neck and wrists. You might never escape!

Then something soft touches your ear. You hear scratching and the stocks open. Someone has released you, but who was it?

A prime number can only be divided by 1 and itself. The number 9 can be divided by 3, so it is not a prime number.

Go to page 12

You load the arrow in the bow and point it at the dragon. The dragon lowers its head and turns back to the cave. You chose the right arrow!

You follow the dragon into its lair.

Go to page 21

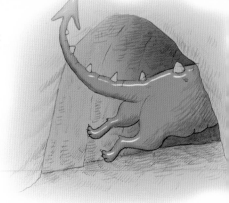

You arrange the disks in order. The missing number should be clear!

1   5   9   ?   17   21

If you think the missing number is 13, go to page 28

If you think the missing number is 14, go to page 31

You blow the horn 6 times and wait. At first nothing happens. Then the boat starts to rock wildly. It's a storm! Lightning flashes and you dive for cover—just in time. A giant wave crashes over the boat. If the wave had caught you, you would have been washed away.

You blew the wrong number! To square a number you must multiply it by itself. What is 3 × 3?

Go to page 10

You've tapped the wrong number! The wolf comes to life! It turns toward you, fangs bared. It's going to bite! Just then something leaps from the mast and knocks you to the deck, just out of the wolf's reach.

A factor of a number divides into that number a whole number of times without any remainder. 10 is a factor of 20, but 12 is not.

Go to page 39

In the office is a set of video screens. On the first you can see the open security shutters, on the second the thieves are drilling into a giant safe, and on the third you can see inside the safe. The Golden Hoard is still inside. There is time to rescue it!

Below the screens you see a burglar alarm panel—the thieves must have found out the code to turn it off. And on the desk is a panel of three colored buttons—one red, one black, one blue. A label above them says "Museum Security." One button controls the security shutters, one button turns the power in the exhibition on and off, and one button sets off the alarm. But which one does what?

You must press the buttons in the right order. If you set off the alarm, or turn off the power, before closing the shutters, the thieves will be warned and escape with the Hoard!

Which button should you press first? Then Pythagorgpuss starts pawing at your bag with a loud "meow!" That's it—the objects you collected! They must hold the clue!

Go to page 35

Number Words

Decimal

Decimal means "made from groups of ten." The decimal number 12.5 has 1 ten, 2 ones, and 5 tenths. The digit after the decimal point is not a whole number but a fraction. The decimal fraction 0.6 is the same as "six tenths" or $\frac{6}{10}$.

Digit

A digit is any one of the following: 0, 1, 2, 3, 4, 5, 6, 7, 8, 9. The number 1953 has four digits: 1, 9, 5, and 3.

Doubles

When you double a number you multiply it by 2. This is the same as adding the number to itself. For example:

double eight = 2 × 8 = 16
double eight = 8 + 8 = 16

Practice working out the doubles by choosing a number, then doubling it again and again.

Double 3 = 6, double 6 = 12, double 12 = 24, double 24 = 48…

Even Number

An even number can be divided by 2 without leaving any remainder. Even numbers are multiples of 2.

2, 4, 6, 8, 10…are even numbers
1, 3, 5, 7, 9, 11…are odd numbers

Factor

A factor is a number that you can divide into another number without leaving a remainder. For example, 3 divides into 12 four times with no remainder. We say that 3 is a factor of 12. What other factors does 12 have?

Fraction

A fraction is a number that describes the parts of a whole. The bottom part of the fraction describes the number of equal parts the whole is divided into and the top part tells you how many parts you have. Half a pizza is less than a whole pizza.

The fraction $\frac{3}{10}$ means that the whole is divided into ten equal parts and we have three of these parts. We can also write fractions as decimal fractions (0.3 in this case).

Three tenths $(\frac{3}{10})$ of the shape is gray.

Hexagon

A hexagon is a plane (flat) shape with six sides.

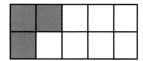

Magic Square

A magic square is made of rows and columns of numbers. If you add the numbers in any row, column, or diagonal, the answer is always the same. The magic number for this square is 30.

Multiple

When you multiply 4 by 3, the answer is 12. We say that 12 is a multiple of 4 and 3. All the multiples of 4 are given by the 4 multiplications table: 4, 8, 12, 16, 20, and so on. All the multiples of 3 are given by the 3 multiplications table: 3, 6, 9, 12…

Number Line

A number line shows numbers spaced out evenly in order. It is useful for comparing one number with another. From this line we can see that 50 is halfway between 0 and 100, so 50 is half the size of 100. Number lines can also help us with calculations.

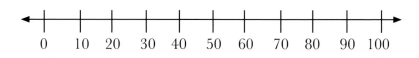

Number Sequence

A number sequence is a list of numbers produced by a rule. The rule might be "add 3 to make the next number" or "subtract 5."

Number Sequence	Rule
5 8 11 14 17 20 23…	add 3
50 45 40 35 30 25 20…	subtract 5
2 8 14 20 26 32 38…	add 6

Odd Number

Odd numbers are 1, 3, 5, 7, 9, 11, and so on. When an odd number is divided by 2, there is always a remainder of 1.

Pentagon

A pentagon is a plane (flat) shape with five sides.

Percentage

A percentage is another way of giving fractions of a whole. One per cent of something is one hundredth part. The symbol for percentage is %. One hundred percent (100 %) is the whole. Fifty percent (50 %) is fifty hundredths, which is the same as one half. Ten percent (10 %) is ten hundredths, which is one tenth. When you divide something into parts, the percentages of the different parts must all add up to 100 %—the whole.

Place Value

The value of the digits in a number depends on their place. In the number 385.2 the digit 3 is in the hundreds place; 8 is in the tens place; 5 is in the ones place; 2 is in the tenths place. The digits on the left have the higher values, the digits on the right the lower values.

Prime Number

A prime number is any whole number, apart from 1, that can only be divided by 1 and itself without leaving a remainder. The only factors of a prime number are 1 and itself. The first 10 prime numbers are: 2, 3, 5, 7, 11, 13, 17, 19, 23, 29.

Roman Numerals

The ancient Romans did not use decimal numbers. They had a different number system. This table gives some Roman numerals from 1 to 1000.

Decimal Number	Roman Numeral	Decimal Number	Roman Numeral
1	I	30	XXX
2	II	40	XL
3	III	50	L
4	IV	60	LX
5	V	70	LXX
6	VI	80	LXXX
7	VII	90	XC
8	VIII	100	C
9	IX	500	D
10	X	900	CM
20	XX	1,000	M

Rounding

The number 23 rounded to the nearest 10 is 20. The number 4,823 rounded to the nearest ten is 4820; to the nearest hundred it is 4,800; to the nearest thousand it is 5,000. The rule for rounding a number is that the last digit you want to keep is rounded up if the digits you don't want start with 5 or more. The last digit stays the same if the digits you don't want start with a number less than 5.

Square

A square is a plane (flat) shape with four equal sides that meet at right angles.

Square Number

A square number can be arranged as a group of dots in the shape of a square.

You can make all the square numbers by multiplying each whole number by itself. The ^{2} sign means "squared."

$1^2 = 1 \qquad 2^2 = 4 \qquad 3^2 = 9 \qquad 4^2 = 16$

Triangle

A triangle is a plane (flat) shape with three sides.

Notes for Parents and Teachers

The Math Quest series of books is designed to motivate children to develop and apply their math skills through engaging adventure stories. The stories work as games in which the children must solve a series of mathematical problems to make progress toward the exciting conclusion.

The books do not follow a conventional pattern. The reader is directed to jump forward and back through the book according to the answers they give to the problems. If their answers are correct, they make progress to the next part of the story; if they are incorrect the mathematics is explained, before the reader is directed back to try the problem again. Additional support may be found on pages 44 to 47.

To support your child's mathematical development you can:

- Read the book with your child.

- Solve the initial problems and discover how the book works.

- Continue reading with your child until he or she is using the book confidently, following the **Go to** instructions to find the next puzzle or explanation.

- Encourage your child to read on alone. Ask, "What's happening now?" Prompt your child to tell you how the story develops and what problems they have solved.

- Discuss math in everyday contexts: shopping, filling up the car at the gas station, looking at the car mileage and road signs when on journeys, using timetables, following recipes, and so on.

- Have fun making up number sequences and patterns. Count in 2s, 3s, 4s, and 5s and larger steps. Ask multiplication table questions to pass the time on journeys. Count backward in different steps. List doubles, square numbers, and prime numbers. Play "I'm thinking of a number, can you guess it?" games in which you ask questions such as "Is it even or odd?" "Is it bigger than 100?" "How many digits does it have?" and so on.

- Play number-based computer games with your child. These will hold children's interest with colorful graphics and lively animations as they practice basic math skills.

- Most of all, make math fun!